The MAGICAL slow cooker

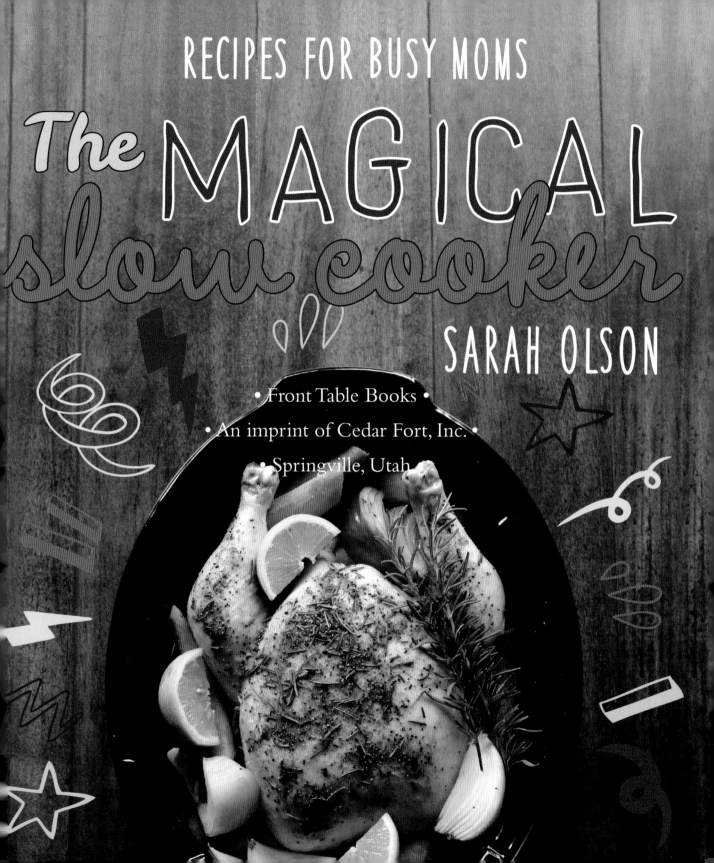

RECIPES FOR BUSY MOMS

The MAGICAL slow cooker

SARAH OLSON

· Front Table Books ·

· An imprint of Cedar Fort, Inc. ·

· Springville, Utah

© 2015 Sarah Olson
Photography on pages 3 and 215 by Annesha Montez

ISBN 13: 978-1-4621-1533-4

Published by Front Table Books, an imprint of Cedar Fort, Inc.
2373 W. 700 S., Springville, UT, 84663
Distributed by Cedar Fort, Inc., www.cedarfort.com

LIBRARY OF CONGRESS CATALOGING-IN-PUBLICATION DATA

Olson, Sarah N., 1982- author.
The magical slow cooker / Sarah N. Olson
    pages cm
Includes index.
ISBN 978-1-4621-1533-4 (acid-free paper)
1. Electric cooking, Slow. I. Title.

TX827.O47 2014
641.5'884--dc23

2014037112

Cover and page design by Bekah Claussen
Cover design © 2015 by Lyle Mortimer
Edited by Justin Greer

Printed in the United States of America

10 9 8 7 6 5 4 3 2 1

Printed on acid-free paper

to my best taste-testers, Chaz and Lola.
you are the loves of my life.

CONTENTS

INTRODUCTION

If you are reading this book, then you must already know the magic your slow cooker holds. Breakfast is ready when you wake. Party food makes you look like a kitchen diva. You can prepare soups, chilies, stews, and main dishes that impress your family and dinner guests. And how about those yummy slow cooker desserts? Cake was meant to be served warm with ice cream!

The last thing I want to do is spend time in the kitchen preparing a meal after working all day. Before I discovered the ease of slow cooking, I would bring home a bucket of chicken or order a pizza more than I'd like to admit. I never feel like the picture of health after having fast food or pizza; I'm unsure if I will wake in the morning, and if I do, I know I can count on heartburn and ill-fitting clothes. Having my slow cooker loaded up in the morning and simmering away while I'm at work keeps me from ordering greasy fast food.

I started my blog, *The Magical Slow Cooker*, in 2013. I wanted a place to keep track of and share my favorite slow cooker recipes. Some of my recipes are lazily simple, and others have a few more ingredients but are still easy to prepare. Most of the ingredients in this book are easy to find at your local grocery store. Who has time to shop at different stores for dinner, anyway? I've included my guide for night-before preparations, so the morning preparations are quick and simple.

ABOUT ME

My mom didn't work outside the home for most of my childhood. She was in the kitchen preparing dinner most of the day, stirring the pasta sauce or soup or making enchiladas from scratch. I applaud her; before I worked full-time I was rarely that organized or patient.

My reality is this: I don't like mornings, and I wait until the last possible moment to get up. Then I have to find my work outfit; part of it is in the dresser, part in the laundry basket on the couch, and part lying wrinkled in the dryer. Then there's my precious daughter Lola Mae. She is five and often refuses to get dressed. After countless times of asking her to, I give in, and she ends up wearing pajamas to Grandma's. I throw a few things that I prepped the night before into my slow cooker, set it, and we're out the door.

I work full-time as a rural mail carrier for the United States Postal Service. You may assume I have the best job, just driving around the countryside in beautiful weather. Though there are great things about living in Oregon, there are probably only ten days out of the year where the weather is a perfect, sunny 72 degrees, which is great for delivering mail. The other days of the year, my right arm is either getting drenched by rain or getting noticeably tanner than my left.

I arrive home anywhere from 3:00 pm to 5:30 pm, depending on how much mail volume there was for the day. Thank goodness for my programmable slow cooker that automatically switches to warm after the cooking time is over. Dinner is prepared when I get home. I may have to make a quick side dish or warm up some bread, but how hard is that?

My husband Chaz is a saint. Right now he is wondering when I am going to get off this computer and help with the laundry (the answer is never). I do need to clean up the kitchen and prep my slow cooker meal for the morning, and then do this all again tomorrow. I wouldn't trade this life for anything; I am truly blessed. I hope you enjoy my family's recipes.

MY SLOW COOKER TIPS

Don't Open the Lid!

First and foremost, don't open that lid! Most slow cooker recipes are meant to be left and forgotten, so there is no need to open the lid and stir (unless the recipe specifies). Every time the lid is opened, moisture and heat are lost. It may take 30 minutes or more for the slow cooker to heat back up.

Dried Beans

Soak dried beans overnight—no exceptions. I do this right in the slow cooker I will be using. Add the beans to the slow cooker, discarding rocks or dirt clumps. Add water until it is 4 inches above the beans. Place the lid on, and let the beans sit in the water for 8–10 hours; don't turn on the slow cooker yet. After they've soaked, drain the water off the beans and continue with the recipe. One last but very important tip about cooking dried beans is not to add the salt until the recipe is done (this can keep the beans from softening).

The "Adding Uncooked Pasta to the Slow Cooker" Debate

This may be personal preference, but I will not add uncooked pasta to my slow cooker. I've tried adding uncooked egg noodles, lasagna noodles, home-style frozen noodles, and wontons. Each meal was thrown in the garbage. It's a texture issue for me: the uncooked pasta turns to mush. And I prefer noodles that are firm and have bite to them. I'm sure there are exceptions, but I will be cooking my noodles separately on the stovetop for my slow cooker dinners.

What Slow Cookers I Use

If I had to choose one slow cooker and give up all the others, I would choose my Crock-Pot brand, 6-quart programmable timer slow cooker. You can make just about every recipe with the 6-quart size. I love the timer that switches to warm after the cooking time is up, which is a dinner-saver; no more overcooked food!

The other sizes of slow cookers I have range from a 2-cup dip size to a 5-quart. I use these for parties only, and they are gathering dust until then.

Optional Night-Before Preparations

If you have busy mornings like I do, you may consider prepping your slow cooker meal the night before. My cutting board is already dirty from cutting bread or slicing green onion for that night's dinner. Here are my tips for prepping as much as you can for the next day's slow cooker dinner so the mornings are less hectic.

Chopping Veggies: Veggies can be chopped the night before and placed in a plastic baggie. Cut potatoes need to be placed in a bowl and covered in water so they don't brown. Place the chopped veggies in the refrigerator. Drain the water off the potatoes before adding them to the slow cooker.

Meats: If the recipe calls for cubed meat and the butcher didn't cube it already for you, this can be done the night before too. Cube the meat, place it into a large plastic baggie, and put the bag in the refrigerator.

Non-Perishable Items: Locate any canned goods and place them on the counter. This is the point when I realize I forgot to buy something and send my husband to the store.

Seasonings: Locating the correct seasonings in my cupboard is not fun first thing in the morning, so I locate the needed seasonings the night before. If there are more than three seasonings that need to be measured for a recipe, I measure them out into a small ramekin or Tupperware for the next morning.

BREAKFAST AND BRUNCH

SALTED CARAMEL APPLE CIDER

Makes 8 servings

This sweet and salty cider is perfect for a fall brunch or for an after-trick-or-treating beverage.

1 (50.7-oz.) bottle Martinelli's apple juice
⅓ cup caramel sauce (jarred ice cream topping)
¼ tsp. ground cinnamon
⅛–¼ tsp. sea salt, to taste
A pinch of nutmeg
2 cinnamon sticks
2 small Gala apples, sliced

Combine everything into a 6-quart slow cooker and stir. Add the salt to taste. Cover and cook on HIGH for 1 hour or until warmed. Serve warm.

WHITE HOT CHOCOLATE

Makes 8 servings

White hot chocolate is great to serve for Christmas parties or for a chilly winter evening.

For the hot chocolate:
½ gallon whole milk
1 (12-oz.) pkg. white chocolate chips
2 tsp. pure vanilla extract
¼ tsp. ground cinnamon
A pinch of nutmeg
A pinch of salt

For the whipping cream:
1 pint heavy whipping cream
1 tsp. pure vanilla extract
2 Tbsp. sugar
A pinch of salt

For serving:
Cinnamon sticks
Ground nutmeg

In a 6-quart slow cooker, add the hot chocolate ingredients. Cover and cook on HIGH for 1½ hours or until hot, occasionally stirring.

With a handheld electric mixer or a stand mixer fitted with the whisk attachment, whip together the heavy whipping cream, vanilla, sugar, and salt until stiff peaks form. Serve the hot chocolate topped with whipped cream and nutmeg and garnish with cinnamon sticks.

MIXED BERRY SYRUP

Makes 8 servings

I often make this the night before I will be making pancakes. This syrup is even great on ice cream!

1 (16-oz.) pkg. fresh strawberries, stemmed and sliced
1 (8-oz.) pkg. fresh raspberries
1 (8-oz.) pkg. fresh blackberries
¼–½ cup sugar (to taste)

Add all the berries to a 3-quart slow cooker. Cover and cook on HIGH for 2 hours without opening the lid during the cooking time. Spoon all contents from the slow cooker into a blender (secure lid well and cover with a towel to prevent possible burning) and pulse until smooth. Add the sugar to taste. Serve warm or chilled.

BREAKFAST WHITE BEANS

Makes 8 servings

Beans for breakfast? If this seems too unusual, try it for dinner! The creamy egg yolks taste so good with the beans and buttered toast.

1 lb. dried white beans
5 cups water
1 cup diced poblano peppers
½ cup diced sweet yellow onion
5 strips bacon, cooked and crumbled
2 chicken bouillon cubes
½ tsp. dried oregano
½ tsp. dried thyme
½ tsp. garlic powder
¼ tsp. pepper
Salt to taste
Bell peppers, eggs, and buttered toast for serving

Soak beans for at least 8 hours before cooking in a 6-quart slow cooker (see page 4 for details). Add the fresh 5 cups of water, poblano, onion, cooked bacon, bouillon cubes, oregano, thyme, garlic powder, and pepper (don't add salt yet), and stir. Cover and cook on LOW for 10 hours. Stir and add salt to taste. Serve topped with sunny-side up eggs and buttered toast.

To make the eggs inside the bell pepper slices, slice bell peppers about ½ inch thick. Spray a pan with nonstick spray and set to medium-high heat. Place peppers in the pan and crack an egg into the pepper. Hold down the pepper with two fingers until the egg starts to set on the bottom. Cover the pan with a lid and cook the eggs to your liking.

CINNAMON APPLESAUCE

makes 8 servings

This applesauce will fill your house with the most amazing aroma; it takes all my willpower not to open the slow cooker and taste while this applesauce is cooking!

4 lbs. apples, any variety
2 cinnamon sticks
2 tsp. ground cinnamon
1 cup water
2 Tbsp. sugar (add to taste)

Peel, core, and cut the apples into ½-inch slices; add them to a 6-quart slow cooker. Add the cinnamon sticks, ground cinnamon, and water. Cover and cook on HIGH for 4 hours (or LOW for 8 hours) without opening the lid during cooking time. Discard the cinnamon sticks. Stir and add the sugar to taste. Serve warm or chilled.

SAUSAGE MUSHROOM FRITTATA

Makes 6 servings

I don't care for eggs that have been slow cooked all night; they tend to dry out. Since I am the first one up in the mornings (even on weekends), it is no problem for me to throw this egg dish in the slow cooker first thing in the morning and have it be ready in time for breakfast.

1 lb. breakfast sausage, browned and drained
½ cup sliced mushrooms
⅓ cup sliced chives or green onion
10 large eggs
⅓ cup milk
¼ tsp. salt
⅛ tsp. pepper
2 cups shredded white cheddar cheese
More chives or green onion for serving

Add the browned sausage, mushrooms, and onions to the bottom of a 6-quart oval slow cooker. In a medium-sized bowl, whisk the eggs, milk, salt, and pepper until smooth. Pour the egg mixture over the sausage, mushroom, and onion. Cover and cook on HIGH for 2 hours and 15 minutes without opening the lid during the cooking time. Add the cheese, cover it, and let it sit until the cheese melts. Top with additional chives or green onion and serve.

GRANOLA BAKED APPLES

Makes 5 servings

These apples are such a treat for breakfast, but they can be served for dessert as well, with a scoop of ice cream or whipped cream.

5 medium-sized Gala apples
1¼ cups granola (I use Bare Naked® Original Cinnamon)
2 Tbsp. melted butter
5 tsp. maple syrup

Cut off the top layer of the apples with a knife. Using a melon ball tool or a round measuring teaspoon, scoop out the core and seeds from each apple. Pack ¼ cup granola into each apple and place into a 6-quart oval slow cooker.

Drizzle the top of the apples evenly with the melted butter and with a teaspoon of maple syrup per apple. Cover and cook on HIGH for 2 to 2½ hours until tender but not falling apart.

RAISIN BREAD FRENCH TOAST CASSEROLE

Makes 6 servings

If someone in your family has an aversion to raisins, get cinnamon swirl bread instead.

1 lb. sliced raisin bread
8 large eggs
2 cups 2% milk
1½ tsp. ground cinnamon
1 tsp. pure vanilla extract
A pinch of salt
Butter and warm maple syrup for serving

Spray a 6-quart oval slow cooker with nonstick spray. Cut the raisin bread slices into quarters and place into the slow cooker. In a medium-sized bowl, whisk the eggs, milk, cinnamon, vanilla, and salt, and then pour over the bread.

With a spatula, squish the bread pieces into the egg mixture, trying to coat each piece. Cover and cook on HIGH for 2 hours and 15 minutes without opening the lid during the cooking time. Serve with butter and warm maple syrup.

HAM BREAKFAST BURRITOS

These burritos are a great on-the-go breakfast or dinner. You can prepare them and wrap them in foil, and then pass them back to your family in the car.

10 eggs
⅓ cup milk
1 cup diced red bell pepper
½ cup diced white onion
2 cups cubed ham
¼ tsp. salt
⅛ tsp. pepper
Tortillas, shredded cheddar cheese, salsa, and avocado for serving

Spray a 6-quart slow cooker with nonstick spray. Whisk the eggs and milk in a large bowl until smooth. Add the bell pepper, onion, ham, salt, and pepper, and stir. Pour into the slow cooker.

Cover and cook on high for 2 hours and 15 minutes without opening the lid during the cooking time.

Using a paper towel, soak up any liquid that accumulated on top. Serve on tortillas topped with shredded cheese, salsa, and avocado.

PEACH BUTTER

Makes 10 servings

You know what I love about peach butter? I don't have to peel the peaches! I can put this peach butter on before I go to bed and wake up to the aroma of peaches and cinnamon.

3 lbs. ripe peaches
1 tsp. cinnamon
Brown sugar to taste
Butter pastries for serving

Slice and quarter the peaches, leaving the skins on and discarding the pits. Add the sliced peaches to a blender and purée; you may need to do this in batches. Add the peach purée and cinnamon to a 6-quart slow cooker and stir. Cover and cook on LOW for 8 hours without opening the lid during the cooking time.

Add the peaches back into the blender (secure the lid well and cover with towel to prevent possible burning) and purée again, adding brown sugar to taste. If the peach butter is too thin, add it back to the slow cooker and cook on LOW for about 30 minutes, uncovered, until it thickens. Serve warm or cold on butter pastries.

PARTY FOOD

ARTICHOKE PARMESAN DIP

Makes 8 servings

You won't see me socializing at a party when this dip is served; I will be stuffing my face until it's gone!

1 (8-oz.) pkg. cream cheese, room temperature
1 cup sour cream
½ cup mayonnaise
1 (1.8-oz.) pkg. leek soup mix
2 garlic cloves, minced
1 Tbsp. lemon juice
¼ tsp. pepper
2 (14-oz.) cans artichokes, drained and chopped
1 (5-oz.) container shredded Parmesan cheese, divided
Sliced French bread for serving

In a large bowl, combine the cream cheese, sour cream, and mayonnaise. Stir in the soup mix, garlic, lemon juice, pepper, artichokes, and half of the cheese. Spray a 4-quart or larger slow cooker with nonstick spray.

Spread the artichoke dip in an even layer and top with the remaining cheese. Cover and cook on HIGH for 1½ hours. Serve with sliced French bread.

BUFFALO WINGS

Makes 6 servings

You won't have to worry about dry wings with this recipe; the wings turn out juicy and tender.

3 lbs. party chicken wings, thawed
1 (12-oz.) bottle Frank's® RedHot® Original sauce
3 Tbsp. salted butter, sliced
Chunky blue cheese dressing
Carrot sticks and celery sticks for serving

In a 4-quart or larger slow cooker, add the chicken, sauce, and sliced butter. Cook on HIGH for 2½ hours.

Preheat the oven to broil at 500 degrees.

Cover a cookie sheet with foil. Using tongs, place the wings on the foiled cookie sheet. Place in the oven for about 10 minutes, until browned, turning the wings halfway through the cooking time. Add the wings back to the slow cooker and stir them back into the sauce. Serve with blue cheese, carrots, and celery.

ROSEMARY PARTY NUTS

Makes 8 servings

Nothing is worse than going to a party where there is nothing to snack on! These nuts are perfect to have on the coffee table for your guests to munch on.

2 (8.75-oz.) cans deluxe mixed nuts
3 Tbsp. melted butter
2 Tbsp. brown sugar
¼ tsp. dried rosemary
½ tsp. cayenne pepper
2 tsp. sesame seeds

Add the nuts to a 3-quart or larger slow cooker. In a small bowl, combine the other ingredients, pour over the nuts, and stir. Cover and cook on HIGH for 1 hour, stirring every 15 minutes, until the nuts are warm and toasty.

Cover a baking sheet with foil and spread nuts out to cool for about 30 minutes. Place the nuts in a bowl for the party.

TACO DIP

Makes 8 servings

Everything you love about tacos in a dip. This dip is perfect for game days.

1 (16-oz.) jar mild salsa
1 (16-oz.) can refried beans
1 (16-oz.) container sour cream
1 (15-oz.) jar nacho cheese
1 lb. ground beef, browned and drained
Salt, pepper, and onion powder to taste
Tortilla chips for serving

Add the salsa, beans, sour cream, and nacho cheese to a 6-quart slow cooker. Season the browned and drained ground beef to taste with salt, pepper, and onion powder. Add the meat to the slow cooker and stir until smooth.

Cover and cook on HIGH for 2 hours, occasionally stirring. Set slow cooker to WARM for the party and serve with tortilla chips.

KIEŁBASA 'N' PEPPERS

Makes 10 servings

The sweetness of the apricot-pineapple preserves compliments the peppers and kiełbasa well in this appetizer.

1 Tbsp. canola or vegetable oil
2 (13-oz.) pkgs. beef kiełbasa, cut into 1-inch slices
1 red bell pepper, cut into 1-inch pieces
1 orange bell pepper, cut into 1-inch pieces
1 white onion, cut into 1-inch pieces
¼ tsp. salt
⅛ tsp. pepper
1 (20-oz.) can pineapple chunks, drained
1 (18-oz.) jar apricot-pineapple preserves

In a large skillet, heat up the oil and brown the kiełbasa, onions, and peppers, and then season with the salt and pepper. Pour this into a 3-quart or larger slow cooker, add the remaining ingredients, and stir. Cover and cook on HIGH for 2 hours, occasionally stirring.

HONEY GARLIC WINGS

Makes 4 servings

These wings are great for parties, but also good for lunch or dinner served over rice.

2 lbs. party chicken wings
⅓ cup soy sauce
⅓ cup honey
3 garlic cloves, minced
¼ tsp. onion powder
1 Tbsp. toasted sesame seeds
2 green onions, sliced

Place the chicken into a 3-quart or larger slow cooker. Combine the soy sauce, honey, garlic, onion powder, and sesame seeds in a small bowl. Pour over the chicken. Cover and cook on HIGH for 2½ hours.

Preheat the oven to broil at 500 degrees. Cover a cookie sheet with foil. Using tongs, place the wings on the foiled cookie sheet. Place in the oven for about 10 minutes, until browned, turning the wings halfway through the cooking time. Add the wings back to the slow cooker and stir them back into the sauce. Top with green onions and serve.

CHEESE FONDUE

Makes 8 servings

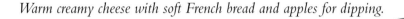

Warm creamy cheese with soft French bread and apples for dipping.

1 (16-oz.) pkg. cheddar cheese, shredded
2 tsp. cornstarch
1 (8-oz.) pkg. cream cheese
1 garlic clove, finely minced
½ cup milk, plus more to thin
French bread cubes and green apple slices for serving

Spray a 2½-quart or larger slow cooker with nonstick spray. Add the cheese and cornstarch and stir. Add the cream cheese, garlic, and milk. Cover and cook on LOW for 1 to 1½ hours, stirring often. More milk may be added to thin out the cheese. Serve with French bread cubes and sliced apples.

Note: Be sure to buy a block of cheese and shred it yourself. A pre-shredded cheese won't melt as well.

ITALIAN BEEF SLIDERS

Makes 10 servings

Diced tomatoes and spaghetti sauce mix make a delicious sauce for these sliders. Served on crusty sourdough bread rolls with melted mozzarella.

1 (3.5-lb.) beef chuck roast
¼ tsp. salt
⅛ tsp. black pepper
2 Tbsp. canola or vegetable oil
1 (1.5-oz.) packet dry spaghetti sauce mix
1 (14.5-oz.) can petite diced tomatoes
½ cup diced white onion
20 sourdough dinner rolls
½ cup olive oil
1 garlic clove
8 ounces mozzarella cheese, sliced

Season the roast with the salt and pepper. In a skillet set to medium-high heat, add the oil and brown the roast on all sides. Add the roast to the slow cooker and add spaghetti sauce mix, tomatoes, and onion. Cover and cook on LOW for 8 hours.

Shred the meat with two forks, discarding any fat; stir meat into the sauce. Cut the dinner rolls down the middle and place on a baking sheet. Brush the olive oil onto the cut sides of the rolls with a pastry brush. Set the oven to broil at 500 degrees. Place the rolls under the broiler and cook for 5–10 minutes, until golden brown. Remove the rolls from the oven, cut the tip off the garlic clove, and rub the browned part of the rolls with the cut garlic clove. Set the tops aside.

Add the shredded meat and sauce to the bottom halves of the rolls and top with cheese. Place under the broiler for 5–10 more minutes, until the cheese melts. Add the tops to the sliders and place on a serving tray.

FIREBALLS

Makes 10 servings

My sister-in-law worked at a restaurant in town that served a secret spicy sauce over crispy tater tots. She watched the cooks make the sauce one day and gave me the recipe, and now I can put this secret spicy sauce on everything!

1½ cups sweet chili sauce
¼ cup Sriracha hot chili sauce
1 (28-oz.) bag frozen original-style precooked meatballs
Snipped chives for serving

In a 6-quart oval slow cooker, stir together the sweet chili sauce and the Sriracha sauce. Add the meatballs and stir. Cover and cook on HIGH for 3 hours, occasionally stirring after the 2-hour mark. Serve topped with the snipped chives.

NACHO BAR

Makes 10 servings

This nacho bar isn't so much a recipe but a fun party idea. When we received an invite to my niece's high school graduation party, my sister-in-law noted that she would be serving a nacho bar for dinner. I waited for weeks in anticipation of this nacho bar. My sister-in-law served 75 people with her nacho bar. The great thing about the nacho bar idea is that you can easily customize it for how many people you are expecting. This may seem like too much nacho cheese for 10 people, but it is more practical than buying a lot of little jars.

1 (6-lb.) can nacho cheese
3 lbs. ground beef, browned and drained
2 (15-oz.) cans black beans, drained
2 (16-oz.) containers sour cream
1 (16-oz.) jar salsa
2 (3.8-oz.) cans sliced olives, drained
1 (12-oz.) jar sliced jalapeños, drained
2 cups diced tomato
2 cups sliced green onion
2 cups guacamole (recipe below)
2–3 large bags tortilla chips

For the guacamole:
4 avocados
¼ cup sour cream
1 Tbsp. lime juice
Salt to taste

Start by adding the nacho cheese sauce into a 6-quart slow cooker. Cover and cook on HIGH for 1–1½ hours, occasionally stirring. After the nacho cheese is warmed, switch the slow cooker to WARM. Add the browned and drained beef to a 3-quart or larger slow cooker, season with salt and pepper to taste, and set to WARM.

To make the guacamole, peel and pit the avocados. Cut them into cubes and place into a small bowl and add the sour cream and lime juice. With the back of a fork, smash the avocados and stir everything together. Add salt to taste.

Add the rest of the ingredients into serving bowls. I use paper boats for serving that can be bought at Costco, but paper plates work fine too.

EASY SALSA

Makes 10 servings

This salsa is very easy to make. The slow cooker "roasts" the vegetables and the blender does the chopping!

1 (14.5-oz.) can diced tomatoes
5 Roma tomatoes, kept whole
1 jalapeño, stem removed
2 garlic cloves, peeled
1 large white onion, peeled and quartered
1 bunch cilantro
½ cup sliced green onion
⅓–½ teaspoon salt, to taste
Tortilla chips for serving

In a 6-quart or larger slow cooker, add the canned diced tomatoes, whole Roma tomatoes, jalapeño, garlic cloves, and onion. Cover and cook on HIGH for 1½ hours.

Cut the cilantro stems off right where the leaves start and discard stems.

Ladle everything from the slow cooker into a blender and add cilantro leaves (secure the lid well and cover with towel to prevent possible burning). Pulse the blender until everything is evenly chopped up. Stir in green onions and add salt to taste. Refrigerate until cold and serve.

SIDE DISHES

FRESH GREEN BEANS, TATERS, AND BACON

Makes 8 servings

I make this side dish for family reunions and barbecues. It goes with any cut of meat and is a crowd pleaser.

5 cups diced russet potatoes
1 lb. fresh green beans, ends snipped, halved
1 cup water
2 chicken bouillon cubes
8 strips bacon, cooked and crumbled
1 tsp. salt
1 tsp. onion powder
½ tsp. garlic powder
⅛ tsp. pepper

Add everything to a 6-quart slow cooker and stir. Cover and cook on HIGH for 3 hours without opening the lid during cooking time.

CALICO BARBECUE BEANS

Makes 10 servings

Barbecue beans are a must for summer get-togethers. This recipe comes together quickly and is great alongside anything barbecued.

2 (28-oz.) cans pork and beans
1 (15.25-oz.) can kidney beans, drained
1 (15-oz.) can butter beans, drained
1 cup barbecue sauce (I use Sweet Baby Ray's)
1 Tbsp. mustard
1 Tbsp. brown sugar
2 Tbsp. minced white onion
6 strips bacon, cooked and crumbled

Combine all the ingredients in a 5 quart or larger slow cooker; stir. Cover and cook on HIGH for 2½ hours, occasionally stirring.

COUNTRY SCALLOPED POTATOES

Makes 6 servings

Once you have tried these homemade scalloped potatoes, you will never go back to the boxed version.

1 (16-oz.) container sour cream
2 cups shredded sharp cheddar cheese
8 strips bacon, cooked and crumbled
1 tsp. onion powder
¼ tsp. salt
⅛ tsp. pepper
4 cups russet potatoes, unpeeled and sliced ¼-inch thick
Paprika for garnish

In a medium-sized bowl, mix the sour cream, cheese, bacon, onion powder, salt, and pepper until smooth. Add the potatoes to this mixture and stir them until coated evenly. Spray a 6-quart slow cooker with nonstick spray.

Spread the potato mixture into the bottom of the slow cooker in an even layer. Cover and cook on HIGH for 3½ hours or until potatoes are tender, sprinkle with paprika, and serve.

REFRIED-STYLE BEANS

I chose not to fry these beans; I don't need more added fat to my Mexican meals. I put these beans in a blender to make them smooth, but you can also use a potato masher.

1 lb. dried pinto beans
5 cups water
½ cup diced white onion
1 large ham hock
½ tsp. oregano
¼ tsp. onion powder
1 bay leaf
½–1 tsp. salt to taste
Shredded cheddar cheese for serving

Soak beans overnight (see page 4 for details). In the morning, drain the water off the beans and add the fresh 5 cups of water, onion, ham hock, oregano, onion powder, and bay leaf (don't add the salt yet). Cover and cook on LOW for 10 hours without opening the lid during cooking time. Discard ham hock and bay leaf.

Add all the beans to a blender and add a few ladles of the broth to the beans, just enough to get the blender moving. You may not need all the liquid. Secure the lid well and cover with towel to prevent possible burning; pulse until smooth. Add the salt to taste, pour into a serving dish, and top with cheese if desired.

SMASHED RED POTATOES

Makes 10 servings

Talk about decadent potatoes! The great thing about these smashed red potatoes is they can be prepared before your guests arrive.

3 lbs. red potatoes
2 chicken bouillon cubes
1 (8-oz.) pkg. cream cheese
¼ cup salted butter
1½ tsp. salt
¼ tsp. pepper
¼ tsp. onion powder

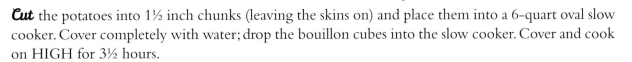

Cut the potatoes into 1½ inch chunks (leaving the skins on) and place them into a 6-quart oval slow cooker. Cover completely with water; drop the bouillon cubes into the slow cooker. Cover and cook on HIGH for 3½ hours.

Using potholders, remove the insert from the slow cooker unit, shift the lid just a bit, and hold it with your thumbs through the potholders. Pour out the water down the kitchen sink. Put the insert back into the slow cooker unit. Place the cream cheese and butter into the potatoes. Cover and let the cream cheese and butter melt for 10 minutes.

Sprinkle the potatoes with the salt, pepper, and onion powder. Using a potato masher, mash the potatoes and stir everything together. Place the potatoes on WARM until ready to serve, up to 2 hours, occasionally stirring. Add a splash of milk if potatoes start to thicken.

ROASTED BEETS

Makes 4 servings

Beets are my favorite salad topping, and they are even better when they are freshly roasted.

4 large beets, stems removed
1 cup Italian dressing
1 cup water

Place the beets in the bottom of a 6-quart slow cooker; add the Italian dressing and water. Cover and cook on LOW for 5–6 hours until tender. Place the beets in a colander and rinse under cold water.

While the water is running over the beets, rub the skins off with your hands. Slice and serve over your favorite salad or eat plain!

SLOW COOKER GREEN BEAN CASSEROLE

Makes 20 servings

For the holidays, my family can't live without green bean casserole, and we need a lot. There is never room in the oven, so I created this slow cooker version. It can simmer while the turkey cooks, and then be thrown in the oven to toast the fried onion topping while the turkey is being carved.

3 (10.75-oz.) cans cream of mushroom soup
½ cup milk
⅛ tsp. pepper
⅛ tsp. onion powder
10 (14.5-oz.) cans cut green beans, drained well
2 (6-oz.) cans French fried onions

In an extra-large bowl, combine the cans of soup, milk, pepper, and onion powder until smooth. Fold in the green beans and one can of French fried onions. Spray a 6-quart slow cooker with non-stick spray and spread the green bean mixture into an even layer. Cover and cook on HIGH for 2½ hours without opening the lid during cooking time.

Preheat oven to 350 degrees. Sprinkle the remaining can of French fried onions over the green bean casserole. Place the slow cooker insert into the oven without the lid on for about 10 minutes, until the onions are browned. Place the insert back to the slow cooker, cover, and set to WARM until ready to eat.

PEPPERED MUSHROOM STEAK TOPPER

Makes 8 servings

Top your grilled steak with these buttery seasoned mushrooms. They take just a few minutes to prepare and taste so good with each bite of steak.

½ lb. small button mushrooms
½ cup salted butter
1½ Tbsp. Montreal steak seasoning
2 garlic cloves, minced

Place the stick of butter into the bottom of a 4-quart slow cooker and add the other ingredients on top. Cover and cook on HIGH for 2 hours without opening the lid during the cooking time. Serve mushrooms and sauce over grilled steaks or chicken.

CREAMY MAC AND CHEESE

Makes 6 servings

My mom and I fell in love with slow cooker mac and cheese a few years ago. My mom likes minced white onion in her recipe and I leave it out.

2 cups dried elbow macaroni
1 (8-oz.) pkg. cream cheese, room temperature
2 cups milk
1 tsp. salt
¼ tsp. black pepper
A pinch of ground nutmeg
4 cups shredded sharp cheddar cheese

Wait to boil the macaroni until you have the other ingredients ready, for the macaroni gets stirred into the sauce while it's still piping hot. In a large bowl, combine the room temperature cream cheese and milk with a whisk (lumps are okay; they will melt when the noodles are added). Stir in the salt, pepper, nutmeg, and cheese.

Add the noodles to boiling water and cook for 8 minutes only. Drain and immediately add to the cheese sauce mixture and stir. Spray a 6-quart slow cooker with nonstick spray; pour macaroni mixture in the slow cooker. Cover and cook on LOW for a 2½ hours.

GARLIC-ROASTED ONE-BITE POTATOES

Makes 8 servings

The farmers market in our area always has fun and unique varieties of veggies. These one-bite potatoes cook up so well in the slow cooker, they turn out creamy on the insides!

3 lbs. one-bite potatoes
¼ cup olive oil
¼ cup water
3 garlic cloves, minced
½ cup white onion
1 tsp. dried basil
½ tsp. salt
⅛ tsp. black pepper

Spray a 6-quart slow cooker with nonstick spray. Add everything to the slow cooker and stir. Cover and cook on HIGH for 3 hours.

CORN ON THE COB

Makes 8 servings

Cooking corn in the slow cooker makes for extra-tender corn, and it stays warm until dinner is ready.

8 ears corn, any variety
1½ cups water
Butter for serving
Salt and pepper to taste

Shuck the corn, halve, and place into a 6-quart slow cooker; add the water. Cover and cook on HIGH for 3 hours without opening the lid during the cooking time. Serve with butter, salt, and pepper.

EASY NON–SLOW COOKER SIDES

Don't have a second slow cooker? Need a quick side to go with your slow cooker dinner? Here are my favorite easy sides:

» steamed rice (in my mind, slow cooker and rice cooker are best friends)

» steamed veggies, such as broccoli, zucchini, asparagus, sugar snap peas, edamame, green beans, and carrots

» frozen Steam n' Mash potatoes

» boxed instant stuffing

» canned corn or green beans

» fresh fruit, such as watermelon, cantaloupe, grapes, and strawberries

» raw baby carrots

» French bread, dinner rolls, biscuits, and garlic bread

» canned refried beans

» canned pineapple rings with cottage cheese on top

» green salad or coleslaw kit

SOUPS AND STEWS

"AT THE BEACH" CLAM CHOWDER

Makes 5 servings

My favorite thing to order when we're at the beach is clam chowder. I can make this chowder when I have a craving so I don't have to wait for a coast trip for this beach treat.

1 (32-oz.) container chicken broth
2 Tbsp. cornstarch
1 cup diced leeks
½ cup diced white onion
5 cups peeled and diced white potatoes
1 tsp. dried thyme
⅛ tsp. black pepper
1 (8-oz.) pkg. cream cheese
2 (6.5-oz.) cans minced clams, drained
Oyster crackers and paprika for serving

Combine the chicken broth and the cornstarch in a 6-quart slow cooker until smooth. Add the leeks, onion, potatoes, thyme, and black pepper. Cover and cook on LOW for 8 hours without opening the lid during cooking time.

Add ⅓ of the potatoes and a couple ladles of broth to a blender (secure the lid well and cover with towel to prevent possible burning). Pulse until smooth. Add this mixture back to the slow cooker. Add the drained clams and stir. Serve with oyster crackers and a sprinkle of paprika.

CHICKEN AND DUMPLINGS

Makes 6 servings

Dumplings puff up well in the slow cooker. I often make this instead of chicken noodle soup when a family member is under the weather.

For the soup:
1½ lbs. boneless skinless chicken breasts
6 cups chicken broth
1½ cups sliced carrots
1 cup sliced celery
½ cup diced white onion
1 tsp. dried thyme
½ tsp. dried rosemary
⅛ tsp. pepper

For the dumplings:
2 cups flour
3 tsp. baking powder
¾ tsp. salt
⅓ cup cold butter
1 cup milk
Parsley for garnish (optional)

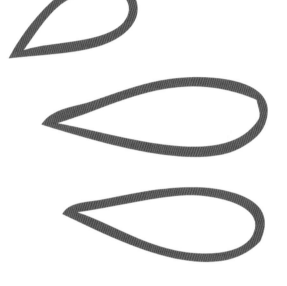

Add the soup ingredients to a 6-quart slow cooker, and stir. Cover and cook on HIGH for 8 hours without opening lid during cooking time. Shred the chicken with two forks and stir.

Mix the flour, baking powder, and salt in a small bowl. Cut the butter into as many small cubes as possible and toss into flour mixture. With the back of fork or a pastry cutter, break up the butter into the flour in smaller pieces.

Add the milk. Combine everything together with clean hands until dough forms. Form the dough into balls (about the size of golf balls) and drop into the hot soup. Cover and cook on HIGH for 1 hour without opening the lid during the cooking time. Garnish with parsley if desired. Serve and enjoy!

FRENCH ONION SOUP

Makes 5 servings

My husband said this was the best soup he has ever tasted. He is hard to trust because he says that about every soup I make. This time I do agree; it is the best soup ever.

3 cups sliced sweet onions
4 Tbsp. salted butter
2 Tbsp. flour
6 cups beef broth
¼ tsp. salt
¼ tsp. sugar
1 tsp. thyme
⅛ tsp. pepper
1 French bread baguette
¼ cup extra virgin olive oil
1 garlic clove
5 slices Swiss cheese

In a large skillet set to medium-high heat, add the butter and onions and cook for 5–7 minutes until browned. Stir in flour and cook for 1 minute more, and then add this onion and flour mixture to a 6-quart slow cooker. Add the beef broth, salt, sugar, thyme, and pepper; stir. Cover and cook on LOW for 8 hours without opening the lid during cooking time.

Slice the baguette into 1-inch slices, place them on a baking sheet, and brush the tops with olive oil. Preheat the oven to broil and place the French bread slices in the oven for 5–10 minutes or until browned. Cut the tip off the garlic clove and rub the garlic clove on the browned bread.

Ladle the soup into oven-proof bowls. Place a piece of the toasted French bread on top of each soup, and then a piece of cheese. Place the bowls on a baking sheet and place under the broiler for 5–10 minutes or until the cheese is bubbly and brown. Place the bowls onto plates and serve with the extra French bread slices on the side.

SPLIT PEA WITH HAM

Makes 6 servings

You either love or hate split pea. I LOVE it! This recipe is great for busy nights; all I have to do when I get home is stir and serve!

1 lb. dried split peas
2 cups diced ham
7 cups chicken broth
1 cup diced carrots
½ cup diced white onion
½ tsp. dried thyme
2 bay leaves
Saltine crackers for serving

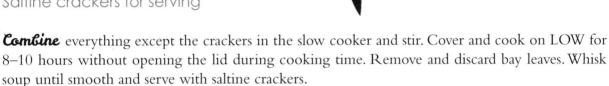

Combine everything except the crackers in the slow cooker and stir. Cover and cook on LOW for 8–10 hours without opening the lid during cooking time. Remove and discard bay leaves. Whisk soup until smooth and serve with saltine crackers.

PASTA E FAGIOLI (PASTA AND BEANS)

Makes 6 servings

An Italian restaurant favorite easily made at home!

1 lb. lean ground beef, browned and drained
1 (32-oz.) container chicken broth
1 (28-oz.) can crushed tomatoes
1 (15-oz.) can white beans, drained
1 (15.25-oz.) can kidney beans, drained
½ cup diced white onion
1½ cup sliced carrots
1 tsp. dried oregano
½ tsp. dried rosemary
½ tsp. salt
1½ cups dried ditalini pasta, cooked according to package directions
Shredded Parmesan and French bread for serving

Add everything except the pasta and serving items to a 6-quart slow cooker. Cover and cook on LOW for 8 hours without opening the lid during cooking time.

Add the drained pasta and stir. Serve the soup topped with Parmesan cheese and French bread for dipping.

CHICKEN TORTILLA SOUP

Makes 5 servings

I make homemade fried tortilla strips for this soup; it makes it over-the-top satisfying.

1 (32-oz.) box chicken broth
1 (14-oz.) can red enchilada sauce
1 (10.75-oz.) can cream of chicken soup
½ cup diced white onion
1 Tbsp. minced jalapeño
¼ cup chopped cilantro
1½ lbs. boneless skinless chicken breasts
10 corn tortillas
Vegetable or canola oil
Salt to taste
Monterey jack cheese and avocado for serving

In a 6-quart slow cooker, combine the chicken broth, enchilada sauce, cream of chicken soup, onion, and jalapeño. Add the chicken breasts into the soup mixture. Cover, and cook on LOW for 8 hours without opening the lid during cooking time.

Cut the corn tortillas into little strips. Heat 1/8 inch of oil in a large skillet set to medium-high heat. Working in batches, add the tortilla strips to the hot oil and stir them with tongs until they are golden brown. Place the tortilla strips on a paper towel to drain and sprinkle with salt to taste.

Shred the chicken in the slow cooker with two forks, add the cilantro, and stir. Serve the soup in bowls topped with tortilla strips, cheese, and avocado.

BEANS AND HAM

Makes 6 servings

What a great fall or winter meal—like love in a bowl.

1 lb. dried Great Northern beans
4 cups chicken broth
1 large ham hock
1 (14.5-oz.) can diced tomatoes
½ cup diced white onion
1 garlic clove, minced
½ tsp. dried thyme
⅛ tsp. black pepper
½–1 tsp. salt (add to taste)
Cornbread for serving

Soak the beans overnight in a 6-quart slow cooker by adding 4 inches of water above the beans (don't turn on the slow cooker). In the morning, drain water off the beans. Add the chicken broth, ham hock, diced tomatoes, garlic, onion, thyme, and pepper. Cover and cook on LOW for 9–10 hours without opening the lid during cooking time. Remove the ham hock to a plate, shred the meat, and add to the slow cooker (discard fat). Add salt to taste. Serve with cornbread.

HAMBURGER SOUP

I could eat this soup once a week, it's that good. Make sure to get dinner rolls for dipping in the soup.

1 lb. extra lean ground beef, cooked and drained
3 cups water
1 (14.5-oz.) can beef broth
1 (6-oz.) can tomato paste
1 (14.5-oz.) can diced tomatoes
1 (14.5-oz.) can cut green beans, drained
4 carrots, sliced
2 celery stalks, sliced
½ cup diced white onion
1 tsp. dried oregano
1 tsp. salt
1 tsp. pepper
1 bay leaf
2 cups dried rotini pasta, cooked according to package directions
Shredded Parmesan cheese and dinner rolls for serving

Add all the ingredients except pasta and serving items to a 6-quart or larger slow cooker; stir. Cook on LOW for 8 hours without opening the lid during cooking time. Discard the bay leaf.

Add the cooked and drained pasta to the slow cooker, stir, and serve with Parmesan cheese and dinner rolls.

BEEF AND BACON MAN STEW

Makes 6 servings

I entered this recipe in the 2013 Crock-Pot Seasoning Mix recipe contest. This recipe for Beef and Bacon Man Stew made it in the top 10 recipes! This stew is rich, hearty, and great topped with sharp cheddar cheese.

2 lbs. stew meat, cubed
6 strips bacon, cooked and crumbled
1 (7-oz.) can Ortega fire-roasted diced green chiles
2 lbs. russet potatoes, sliced into thick half rounds
1 large white onion, diced
2 garlic cloves, minced
1 (14-oz.) can beef broth
1 (6-oz.) can tomato paste
1 (1.5-oz.) pkg. Crock-Pot Hearty Beef Stew Seasoning Mix
1 (15.2-oz.) can whole kernel corn
Shredded sharp cheddar cheese for serving

Add the stew meat, bacon, green chiles, potatoes, onion, and garlic cloves to a 6-quart slow cooker. In a small bowl, whisk together the beef broth, tomato paste, and seasoning mix until smooth; pour over contents in the slow cooker.

Cover and cook on LOW for 8 hours. Stir in the drained corn and serve each bowl topped with shredded cheese.

LEFTOVER TURKEY NOODLE SOUP

Makes 8 servings

After Thanksgiving dinner, my mom always sends me home with a Ziploc bag of turkey. I usually have to work the next day, barely functioning after spending the entire day with the extended family. This soup is just what I need to transform those turkey leftovers; it tastes just like my grandma made it.

7 cups chicken stock
3 cups cooked leftover turkey or chicken, shredded
1 cup sliced carrots
1 cup sliced celery
1 cup white onion
1 tsp. dried thyme
2 bay leaves
⅛ tsp. black pepper
½ lb. dried fettuccine noodles, cooked according to package directions
Salt and pepper to taste

Add the chicken broth, turkey, carrots, celery, onion, thyme, bay leaves, and pepper to a 6-quart or larger slow cooker. Cover and cook on LOW for 8 hours without opening the lid during cooking time.

Add the drained cooked noodles to the slow cooker, cover, and let cook for 1 more hour. Remove bay leaves and serve.

LIGHTENED-UP BAKED POTATO SOUP

Makes 4 servings

Baked potato soup is awesome, but not for my waistline. Some baked potato soup is served buffet-style, where you top your own bowl with sour cream, cheese, bacon, and onions. But I have a serious problem with portion control, so I created this recipe with reduced-fat toppings mixed in: problem solved!

1 (32-oz.) box chicken broth
4 cups peeled and diced russet potatoes
½ cup diced white onion
½ cup cream cheese (⅓ less fat)
4 strips turkey bacon, cooked and sliced
1 cup shredded reduced-fat cheddar cheese
Chives or green onions for serving

Add the chicken broth, potatoes, and onion to a 6-quart slow cooker. Cover and cook on LOW for 8 hours without opening the lid during cooking time.

Ladle out half of the potatoes and a few ladles of broth into a blender, add the cream cheese, (secure the lid well and cover with towel to prevent possible burning), and pulse until smooth. Add this mixture back into the slow cooker and stir.

Add the bacon and cheese to the slow cooker and stir. Ladle into bowls for serving and top with chives or green onions.

CHILIES

STEAK TACO CHILI

Makes 6 servings

This chili is different than most; I stir in fresh-style store-bought salsa at the end of the cooking time. This gives the chili a slight crunch and great depth of flavor.

2 lbs. beef top sirloin or stew meat, cubed
2 (14.5-oz.) cans beef broth
1 (6-oz.) can tomato paste
2 (15-oz.) cans kidney beans, drained
1 (1.25-oz.) packet dry taco seasoning mix
1 (16-oz.) container fresh salsa (refrigerator section of store)
Shredded cheddar cheese, sour cream, and corn chips for serving

In a 6-quart or larger slow cooker, add the beef, beef broth, tomato paste, beans, and taco mix; stir. Cover and cook on LOW for 8 hours without opening the lid during cooking time. Stir in the fresh salsa and serve with desired toppings.

V8 CHILI

Makes 10 servings

When I first started dating my husband, he made me this chili and garlic bread. This chili was so good; I had to marry this man, because he knew how to cook! Later I found out this was the extent of his cooking skills. On a lighter note, I can always guess what we are having for dinner when it's his night to cook.

2 (14.5-oz.) cans stewed tomatoes
2 lbs. lean ground beef, browned and drained
1 (46-oz.) can V8 juice
2 (15.25-oz.) cans kidney beans, drained
2 (1.25-oz.) pkgs. dry chili mix
1 cup diced white onion
¼ tsp. onion powder
¼ tsp. salt
¼ tsp. pepper
Shredded cheddar cheese, diced onion, and garlic bread for serving

Pour the 2 cans of stewed tomatoes in a 6-quart slow cooker, take a butter knife, and cut the stewed tomato chunks into bite-sized pieces. Add the browned, drained ground beef, V8 juice, drained kidney beans, chili mix, diced onion, onion powder, salt, and pepper. Stir.

Cover and cook on LOW for 8 hours without opening the lid during cooking time. Serve topped with cheese and onions and with garlic bread on the side.

COWBOY CHILI BEANS

Makes 5 servings

These beans are slightly sweet and are best served with cornbread and butter.

4 (15-oz.) cans pork and beans
2 Tbsp. barbecue sauce
½ cup diced onion
2 tsp. chili powder
¼ tsp. onion powder
¼ tsp. garlic powder
1 lb. ground beef, browned and drained
Salt and pepper to taste
Cornbread and butter for serving

Add the pork and beans, barbecue sauce, onion, chili powder, onion powder, and garlic powder to a 6-quart slow cooker.

Season the browned and drained ground beef with salt and pepper to taste, and add to the slow cooker.

Cover and cook on LOW for 5 hours without opening the lid during the cooking time. Serve with cornbread and butter.

"NO CAN" TURKEY CHILI

Makes 8 servings

Most slow cooker meals contain a lot of canned ingredients. I created this chili for a healthy mid-week dinner.

1½ cups dried red beans
5 cups water
1¼ lbs. 7% fat ground turkey, browned and drained
1 poblano pepper, diced
1 red or yellow bell pepper, diced
2 celery stalks, sliced
½ cup diced red onion
1 garlic clove, minced
3 Tbsp. chili powder
½ tsp. onion powder
⅛ tsp. pepper
½–1 tsp. salt (to taste)
Diced red onion and cheese for serving

The night before, soak the beans by placing the dried beans into a 6-quart slow cooker. Cover with 4 inches of water and let the beans soak overnight without turning the slow cooker on.

In the morning, drain the water and add the fresh 5 cups of water along with the rest of the ingredients (except salt and toppings).

Cover and cook on LOW for 9 hours without opening the lid during cooking time.

Add the salt to taste and top with desired toppings.

WHITE BEAN CHICKEN CHILI

Makes 8 servings

A friend of mine makes the best chicken chili. I did my best to replicate it here, and boy is it good!

2 (14.5-oz.) cans chicken broth
1 (10.75-oz.) can cream of chicken soup
1 (14.5-oz.) can diced tomatoes
2 (15-oz.) cans great northern beans, drained
1 (15.25-oz.) can whole kernel corn, drained
1 (4-oz.) can fire-roasted green chiles
1 (1.25-oz.) pkg. white chicken chili seasoning mix
½ cup diced white onion
2 lbs. boneless skinless chicken breasts
Monterey Jack cheese and green onion for serving

Mix the chicken broth and cream of chicken soup in a 6-quart slow cooker until smooth. Add the diced tomatoes, beans, corn, chiles, seasoning mix, onion, and chicken breasts.

Cover and cook on LOW for 8 hours without opening the lid during cooking time.

Shred the chicken with 2 forks and stir. Top each serving with cheese and green onion.

FRITO PIES

Makes 8 servings

I bring this meal into my work for parties, and everyone goes crazy for it!

2 lbs. ground hamburger, browned and drained
3½ cups water
1 (15-oz.) can Ro-Tel Diced Tomatoes & Green Chilies
1 (14.5-oz.) can diced tomatoes
2 (15-oz.) cans pinto beans, drained
2 (1.25-oz.) pkgs. dry taco seasoning mix
1 (6-oz.) can tomato paste
8 (2-oz.) bags Fritos (or 1 large bag)
Shredded cheddar cheese and diced white onion for servings

Add the browned and drained beef, water, Ro-Tel, diced tomatoes, pinto beans, taco seasoning, and tomato paste to a 6-quart slow cooker; stir.

Cover and cook on LOW for 8 hours without opening the lid during cooking time.

Stir and serve over Fritos, topped with cheese and onion.

CHILI DOGS

Regular chili to chili dogs in minutes.

1 entire chili recipe from page 114
8 beef hot dogs
8 hot dogs buns
Toppings such as shredded cheddar cheese, onion, mustard, and hot peppers

After the chili has cooked for 8 hours on LOW, add the hot dogs into the chili and cook for 20–30 more minutes on LOW, until the hot dogs are warmed.

Serve on buns with desired toppings.

MAIN DISHES

SOUR CREAM BEEF STROGANOFF

Makes 5 servings

This stroganoff recipe is one of the first recipes of my mom's that I adapted for the slow cooker. My mom made her version with ground beef on the stovetop. I make this slow cooker version with stew meat, and my recipe has very little active prep time.

2 lbs. cubed beef stew meat
½ cup diced white onion
2 cups sliced mushrooms
2 (1.25-oz.) pkgs. brown gravy dry mix
1½ cups water
1½ cups sour cream
Cooked egg noodles or steamed rice and additional sour cream for serving

Add the stew meat, onions, and mushrooms to a 4-quart or larger slow cooker.

Whisk the gravy mixes and the water in a small bowl; pour this into the slow cooker.

Cover and cook on LOW for 8 hours without opening the lid during cooking time.

Stir in the 1½ cups sour cream and ladle the stroganoff sauce over noodles or rice.

Top with more sour cream for garnish.

EASY ASIAN BEEF

Makes 4 servings

I love Chinese food at home, but I never have the long line of ingredients some recipes call for. This simple Asian beef is very tender and has lots of sauce for the rice to soak up.

1.5 lbs. beef strips (sometimes labeled "stir-fry beef")
1 cup beef broth
⅓ cup barbecue sauce (I use Sweet Baby Ray's)
1 Tbsp. soy sauce
¼ tsp. ground ginger
1 garlic clove, minced
1 Tbsp. cornstarch
Steamed rice and sliced sweet baby peppers for serving

Place the beef in a 4-quart or larger slow cooker.

In a small bowl, whisk together the beef broth, barbecue sauce, soy sauce, ground ginger, garlic, and cornstarch; pour over the beef.

Cover and cook on LOW for 5 hours without opening the lid during cooking time.

Serve over rice topped with sliced sweet baby peppers.

MEATLOAF ONION BOMBS

Makes 6 servings

I put my favorite meatloaf between two onion shells, wrapped them in foil, and cooked them up in my slow cooker. If you're not feeling so ambitious to make these meatloaf bombs, I've included my standard meatloaf recipe below.

3 large eggs
1 cup diced white onion
1 cup diced red or green bell pepper
⅓ cup ketchup
¼ cup milk
¼ tsp. onion powder
½ tsp. salt
½ tsp. pepper
25 saltine crackers
2 lbs. 10%-fat ground beef
2 large white onions

In a large bowl add the eggs, onion, bell pepper, ketchup, milk, onion powder, salt, and pepper. Crush the saltine crackers over the bowl in your hands; mix this together with a spoon. Add the ground beef and combine with a clean hand, mixing only until it comes together.

Prepare the onion shells by cutting off both ends of the onion and cutting down the middle; separate the onion shells into matching pairs. Fill half an onion shell with meatloaf mixture, fill the matching onion shell, and connect them. Repeat this until meatloaf mixture is gone.

Wrap each meatloaf bomb in foil twice and place into a 6-quart slow cooker. Cover and cook on HIGH for 5 hours only, without opening the lid during cooking time. Serve promply, for the meatloaf will continue to cook in the foil.

Standard Meatloaf Recipe: Follow recipe above, but instead of filling the onion shells, shape the meat into a loaf shape in 6-quart slow cooker that has been sprayed with nonstick spray. Cover and cook on LOW for 5 hours. If desired, add the sauce from page 158 during the last 10 minutes.

TEXAS PEACH BARBECUE SANDWICHES

Makes 6 servings

I sweetened a store-bought barbecue sauce with peach preserves. I serve this peach barbecue beef on Texas toast and top with coleslaw.

1 (3-lb.) beef chuck roast
1¾ cup barbecue sauce
¾ cup peach preserves
1 cup water
Texas toast slices, coleslaw cabbage mix, and coleslaw dressing for serving

Place the beef roast into a 6-quart slow cooker.

In a small bowl, mix the barbecue sauce and peach preserves together. Pour half of the peach barbecue sauce over the roast and refrigerate the remainder of the peach barbecue sauce. Pour the water around the roast.

Cover and cook on LOW for 8 hours without opening the lid during cooking time.

Lightly toast the bread in a toaster.

Mix just enough coleslaw dressing into the cabbage mix to make it moist.

Shred the meat with two forks.

Assemble the sandwiches, topping with reserved peach barbecue sauce and coleslaw.

SALSA STEAK BURRITOS

Makes 4 servings

I serve this salsa steak on uncooked-style tortillas (they are in the refrigerated section of the store near the cheese). They are easily browned in a dry skillet, and they taste just like homemade.

2 Tbsp. vegetable or canola oil
1½–2 lbs. top sirloin, cut into 1-inch cubes
⅛ tsp. salt
⅛ tsp. pepper
⅛ tsp. onion powder
1 (16-oz.) jar mild Pace Picante salsa
8 Tortilla Land tortillas, cooked according to package directions
Sour cream for serving

In a large skillet set to medium-high, add the oil and the sirloin. Season the meat with salt, pepper, and onion powder.

Brown the meat on all sides—no need to cook through. Add the salsa to the pan and with a spatula scrape up any meaty bits from the bottom of the pan. Add the meat and salsa to a 3-quart or larger slow cooker.

Cover and cook on HIGH for 3 hours without opening the lid during cooking time.

Serve on the cooked tortillas and top with sour cream.

ALL-DAY MEAT SAUCE

Makes 6 servings

My mom would simmer her meat sauce on the stove most of the day. She would have to stop by the stove and stir every once in a while. No stirring my slow cooker version; just set it and go on with your day!

1 lb. ground beef, browned and drained
1 (28-oz.) can crushed tomatoes
2 (14-oz.) cans diced tomatoes
1 (6-oz.) can tomato paste
2 Tbsp. brown sugar
½ cup diced white onion
1 garlic clove, minced
1 Tbsp. dried oregano
2 tsp. dried basil
¼ tsp. black pepper
¾ tsp. salt
A pinch of red pepper flakes
Cooked noodles and Parmesan cheese for serving

Place everything except noodles and Parmesan cheese in a 6-quart slow cooker and stir.

Cover and cook on LOW for 8 hours without opening the lid during cooking time.

Serve over cooked noodles and top with Parmesan cheese.

POT ROAST DINNER

Is there anything homier than a pot roast dinner? This meal has it all: meat, potatoes, carrots, onions, and gravy too! I like to make this meal on Sundays; there is always some left over for Monday lunches.

3–4 lbs. bottom round or chuck beef roast
1 (10.75–oz.) can cream of mushroom
1 (10.75–oz.) can French onion soup
¼ cup cornstarch
1½ lbs. red potatoes, kept whole
6 carrots, peeled and cut in 3 sections
1 large onion, cut into 8 sections
Salt and pepper to taste
Dinner rolls and butter for serving

Place the roast into a 6-quart slow cooker. Whisk together the soups and cornstarch in a small bowl; pour over the roast in the slow cooker. Add the potatoes, carrots, and onion.

Cover and cook on LOW for 8–9 hours without opening the lid during cooking time.

Place the veggies and roast on serving platter, cutting the potatoes into quarters as you place them onto platter. Cover with foil. Take the gravy that is in the slow cooker and pour through a metal strainer into a large bowl. Add salt and pepper to taste. Put the strained gravy into a gravy boat and serve.

POOR MAN'S STEAK DIANE

Makes 6 servings

My favorite thing to order at a restaurant in town is Steak Diane; the sauce has so much depth of flavor. Traditional Steak Diane is made with beef tenderloin; I make this poor man's version with stew meat. This tougher and cheaper cut of meat cooks up tender thanks to my slow cooker.

2 lbs. beef stew meat, cubed
2 (1.25–oz.) pkgs. brown gravy dry mix
1¼ cups water
1½ Tbsp. Dijon mustard
2 Tbsp. tomato paste
¼ tsp. dried thyme leaves
¼ tsp. dried oregano leaves
1 cup sliced mushrooms
¼ cup minced shallot
1 garlic clove, minced
⅓ cup sour cream
Prepared mashed potatoes or steamed rice for serving

Place the stew meat into a 4-quart or larger slow cooker. Mix the rest of the ingredients, except the sour cream, in a medium bowl and pour over stew meat.

Cover and cook on LOW for 8 hours without opening the lid during cooking time.

Add sour cream and stir. Serve over mashed potatoes or steamed rice.

CORNED BEEF, CABBAGE, AND POTATOES

Makes 6 servings

This makes for an easy St. Patrick's Day dinner. (Or any day, for that matter!) The leftover meat can be made into Reuben sandwiches.

3½ lbs. corned beef brisket, flat cut
Pickling spice packet that comes with corned beef
1½ lbs. small red potatoes, kept whole
½ cup water
½ head cabbage
Horseradish mustard for serving

Put the corned beef in a 6-quart or larger slow cooker and sprinkle the pickling spice on top.

Add the potatoes around the edges of the roast. Add the water.

Cover and cook on LOW for 7–8 hours, without opening the lid during the cooking time.

Cut the cabbage into a few pieces and place on top of the corned beef and potatoes. Cook for 1 hour longer or until cabbage is tender.

Serve with horseradish mustard if desired.

TATER TOT CASSEROLE

Makes 8 servings

If you have any kids in the house, don't count on having anything left over with this recipe. It pleases even the pickiest of eaters.

1 (32-oz.) bag frozen tater tots
2 (14.5-oz.) cans cut green beans, drained
1 lb. ground beef
½ cup diced white onion
¼ tsp. salt
⅛ tsp. pepper
2 (10.75-oz.) cans cream of mushroom soup
½ cup milk
2 cups shredded cheddar cheese

Spray a 6-quart slow cooker with nonstick spray. Add the frozen tots to the slow cooker in an even layer.

Brown the ground beef with the onion, drain the fat, and add salt and pepper. Add the cream of mushroom soup and milk to the pan with the beef. Pour this meat mixture over the tots and green beans.

Cover and cook on LOW for 4 hours. Turn off slow cooker, sprinkle cheese evenly over top, and replace lid for 10 minutes or until cheese is melted.

POT ROAST DIPS WITH HORSERADISH CREAM SAUCE

Makes 5 servings

Here I jazzed up the standard beef French dip by serving these pot roast dips on homemade-style buns topped with horseradish cream sauce.

For the roast and au jus:

1 (1-oz.) pkg. au jus dry mix
3 cups water
1 bay leaf
1 garlic clove, minced
1 cup sliced white onion
¼ tsp. salt
¼ tsp. pepper
¼ tsp. onion powder
¼ tsp. garlic powder
2 Tbsp. vegetable or canola oil
2½ lbs. bottom round rump roast

For the horseradish cream sauce:

½ cup sour cream
2 tsp. hot cream horseradish
1 tsp. dried parsley
⅛ tsp. salt
⅛ tsp. pepper
A pinch of onion powder

Homemade-style hamburger buns and Swiss cheese for serving

In a 6-quart slow cooker, mix the au jus mix and water until smooth. Add the bay leaf, garlic, and onion. In a small bowl, mix the salt, pepper, onion powder, and garlic powder. Pat this seasoning mixture evenly onto the roast.

Set a large skillet to medium-high heat. When the pan is hot, add the oil and brown the roast on all sides; no need to cook the meat through. Add the meat to the slow cooker into the au jus.

Cover and cook on LOW for 8 hours without opening the lid during cooking time. In a small bowl, mix the horseradish cream sauce ingredients together until smooth; cover and refrigerate. Remove the meat onto plate and cover in foil. Strain the au jus next. To do this, place a metal strainer over a large bowl; using potholders, remove the insert from the slow cooker unit and pour the juices from the slow cooker through the strainer into the bowl. Place this bowl of au jus in the fridge for 10 minutes. Remove the au jus from the fridge, spoon off the grease (or use a wadded up paper towel), and dab grease off the top of the au jus. Shred the meat with 2 forks. Serve on the buns with cheese and the horseradish cream sauce. Ladle the au jus into little bowls for dipping.

CHICKEN AND GRAVY

Makes 6 servings

This chicken dish is my daughter Lola's favorite slow cooker meal, which makes me happy because getting her to eat isn't always easy. I like to serve this chicken and gravy over mashed potatoes and sourdough bread.

2 lbs. boneless skinless chicken breast
2 (1.25–oz.) pkgs. chicken gravy dry mix
1 (10.75–oz.) can cream of chicken soup
⅛ tsp. pepper
1¾ cup water

Add the chicken to a 3-quart or larger slow cooker.

In a medium-sized bowl, whisk the gravy mixes, soup, pepper, and water. Pour over chicken.

Cover and cook on LOW for 8 hours without opening lid during cooking time. Lightly shred the chicken and stir gravy.

Serve with desired sides.

GREEN CHILE CHICKEN ENCHILADA CASSEROLE

Makes 6 servings

This is the easiest way to make enchiladas. The sauce and chicken simmer all day, and then the enchilada fixings are stirred into the sauce and topped with cheese.

1½ lbs. boneless skinless chicken breasts
1 (10-oz.) can green enchilada sauce
1 (10.75-oz.) can cream of chicken soup
1 (4-oz.) can diced fire-roasted Chile peppers
½ cup sliced green onion
½ cup sour cream
3 cups shredded sharp cheddar cheese, divided
16 corn tortillas, cut into 1×2–inch strips (about 3 cups total)
Corn chips, avocado, sour cream, and green onion for serving

In a 6-quart slow cooker, add the chicken.

In a small bowl, whisk together the enchilada sauce, cream of chicken soup, and peppers. Pour over the chicken in the slow cooker.

Cover and cook on LOW for 8 hours without opening the lid during the cooking time.

Shred the chicken with 2 forks. Stir in the green onion, sour cream, 1 cup cheese, and sliced tortillas, and then pat the mixture down smooth. Top with remaining cheese, cover, and cook on HIGH for 1 hour more. Serve and enjoy!

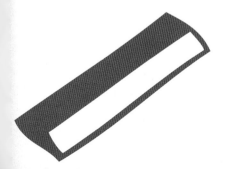

INDIAN BUTTER CHICKEN

Makes 5 servings

Butter Chicken is an Indian dish that is usually flavored with Indian spices, butter, and cream. The jarred butter chicken sauce that you can find at the grocery store has everything you need to flavor the chicken thighs perfectly.

2 lbs. boneless skinless chicken thighs
1 (15-oz.) jar Patak's Butter Chicken Simmer Sauce
Salt and pepper to taste
Steamed rice, and cilantro for serving

Place the chicken thighs in the bottom of a 4-quart or larger slow cooker and cover with the butter chicken simmer sauce.

Cover and cook on LOW for 8 hours.

Serve over steamed rice; season with salt and pepper to taste and top with cilantro if desired.

HONEY MUSTARD CHICKEN SANDWICHES

Makes 5 servings

Tangy mustard and sweet honey shredded chicken sandwiches. I often serve these sandwiches with sweet potato fries.

½ cup yellow mustard
½ cup honey
1 garlic clove, minced
⅛ tsp. pepper
2 lbs. boneless skinless chicken breasts
5 large hamburger buns
5 slices cheddar cheese

In a 3-quart or larger slow cooker, stir together the mustard, honey, garlic, and pepper. Add the chicken breasts and flip them so they get coated on both sides with the sauce.

Cover and cook on LOW for 5 hours without opening the lid during cooking time.

Shred the meat with 2 forks and serve on the toasted buns with cheddar cheese.

LEMON ROSEMARY CHICKEN

Makes 4 servings

Putting a whole chicken in the slow cooker produces the juiciest, tenderest chicken you will ever taste. The veggies are optional, and I've included a couple variations of seasoning below if you don't like rosemary.

1 (4½-lb.) chicken
¼ cup butter, melted
1 lemon
4 carrots, peeled and halved
1 large red onion, peeled and quartered
1 lemon
½ tsp. dried rosemary
½ tsp. salt
¼ tsp. paprika
¼ tsp. garlic powder
⅛ tsp. pepper

Spray a 6-quart slow cooker with nonstick spray. Make 5 balls out of foil and place them in the slow cooker. Remove the neck and any other loose bits from the inside of the chicken and discard. Place the chicken on top of the foil balls and brush on the melted butter. Cut the lemon in half and squeeze all the juice out over the chicken; tuck the lemon halves around the chicken.

In a small bowl, combine the rosemary, salt, paprika, garlic powder, and pepper. Sprinkle evenly over the chicken.

Cover and cook on LOW for 6 hours without opening the lid during the cooking time.

Variations:

LEMON THYME CHICKEN: Substitute ½ teaspoon dried thyme for the rosemary

LEMON CREOLE CHICKEN: Substitute 1½ teaspoons of Tony Chachere's creole seasoning for the rosemary, salt, paprika, garlic powder, and pepper.

CILANTRO LIME DRUMSTICKS

Kids love drumsticks; so do I. I finish off these drumsticks in the oven to get them crispy.

2 small limes
¼ cup chopped cilantro
1 garlic clove, minced
½ tsp. salt
⅛ tsp. pepper
4 lbs. chicken drumsticks

Juice the limes into a 6-quart slow cooker. Add the cilantro, garlic, and salt; stir.

Add the chicken drumsticks and stir to coat the chicken into the sauce.

Cover and cook on HIGH for 2½–3 hours, without opening the lid during the cooking time.

Preheat the oven to broil at 500 degrees. Cover a cookie sheet with foil. Using tongs, place the drumsticks on the foiled cookie sheet. Place in the oven for about 10 minutes until browned, turning the drumsticks halfway.

Serve with juices from the slow cooker.

CHEESY CHICKEN AND BROCCOLI
Makes 5 servings

My daughter isn't a fan of broccoli. With this dish, the broccoli cooks down into the sauce, and she doesn't even realize she is eating it.

1 lb. boneless skinless chicken breasts
2 (10.75-oz.) cans cream of mushroom soup
⅛ tsp. ground pepper
⅛ tsp. onion powder
2 cups broccoli florets
2 cups sliced mushrooms
½ cup diced white onion
2 cups shredded sharp cheddar cheese
Steamed rice and more cheese for serving

Place the chicken on the bottom of a 6-quart slow cooker. Spread the cans of soup over the chicken. Sprinkle with pepper and onion powder. Add the broccoli, mushrooms, and onion in an even layer.

Cover and cook on LOW for 8 hours without opening the lid during cooking time.

Shred the chicken with 2 forks, add the cheese, and stir together. Ladle the chicken and sauce over rice in bowls and top with more cheese if desired.

LEMON CHICKEN SPAGHETTI

Makes 5 servings

This lemon chicken spaghetti is the easiest pasta dish I've ever made (besides boxed mac and cheese). Leftovers are even delicious cold.

1½ lb. raw chicken tenderloins
1 cup Italian dressing (I use Newman's Own "Family Italian Recipe")
Juice of 1 large lemon
½ lb. dried spaghetti noodles, cooked according to package directions
2 cups bite-sized cut asparagus
½ cup grated Parmesan cheese
A pinch of red pepper flakes
More grated Parmesan cheese for serving

Add the chicken, Italian dressing, and lemon juice to a 6-quart slow cooker.

Cover and cook on LOW for 8 hours without the opening lid during cooking time.

Using a butter knife, cut the chicken tenders into bite-sized pieces.

Cook the pasta according to package directions, add the cut asparagus to the boiling water during the last 5 minutes of cooking time, drain the pasta and asparagus, and add to the slow cooker with the chicken and lemon sauce. Add the red pepper flakes and the ½ cup Parmesan cheese and gently stir together. Top with more Parmesan cheese for serving.

TURKEY-STUFFED PEPPERS

These turkey-stuffed peppers recipe are moist and tender. My house smells so good while these are cooking, and I can barely wait to eat them!

For the peppers:
4 bell peppers, any colors
1¼ lbs. 7% fat ground turkey
1 cup cooked rice, cooled
1 egg
½ cup diced bell pepper (leftover from above peppers)
½ cup diced white onion
½ tsp. salt
⅛ tsp. onion powder

For the topping:
1 cup ketchup
1 Tbsp. brown sugar
1 tsp. mustard

Cut the bell peppers down the sides, just over a bit from the stem; set aside. Dice the cut-off portion of the peppers for the filling. Add the ground turkey, cooked rice, egg, bell pepper, onion, salt, and onion powder to a large bowl; mix with your hands to combine. Stuff the filling into the peppers.

Spray a 6-quart slow cooker with nonstick spray and add the stuffed peppers.

Cover and cook on LOW for 5–6 hours. Mix the sauce ingredients in a small bowl and spoon over peppers. Cover and cook on LOW for 15 minutes more.

PORK CARNITAS

This pork carnitas meat is melt-in-your-mouth tender. The homemade pico de gallo salsa gives these tacos a perfect crunch.

For the carnitas:
2½ lbs. pork shoulder, trimmed and cut into 4 pieces
1 (15-oz.) can chicken broth
½ cup onion diced
1 garlic clove, minced
1 bay leaf
1 cinnamon stick
1 Tbsp. chili powder
½ tsp. oregano
¼ tsp. salt
Juice of ½ an orange
Juice of ½ a lime

For the pico de gallo salsa:
3 diced Roma tomatoes
3 Tbsp. diced white onion
1 Tbsp. minced jalapeño
2 tablespoons cilantro leaves, chopped
2 dashes salt
Juice of ½ a lime

Corn or flour tortillas for serving

Place the ingredients for the carnitas into a 6-quart slow cooker.

Cover and cook on LOW for 8 hours without opening the lid during the cooking time. Discard the cinnamon stick. In a small bowl combine the pico de gallo ingredients.

Shred the pork with 2 forks, discarding any fat. Serve on warm tortillas, topped with pico de gallo.

HAM SLICES WITH PINEAPPLE RINGS

Makes 6 servings

This sweet ham is topped with pineapples and cherries. Serve the leftover ham for breakfast the next day.

1 (20-oz.) can pineapple rings (juices reserved for sauce)
3 Tbsp. brown sugar
1 Tbsp. mustard
1 Tbsp. apple cider vinegar
2 ½ lbs. cooked ham
12 maraschino cherries

Add the pineapple juice from the cans of pineapple, brown sugar, mustard, and apple cider vinegar to a 6-quart slow cooker; stir until the mustard and brown sugar dissolve.

Slice the ham into ½ in slices, place into the sauce, and add the pineapple and cherries on top of the ham.

Cover and cook on LOW for 4–5 hours. Serve the ham slices with the pineapple and cherries on top and drizzle the sauce from the slow cooker on top.

CHINESE FIVE SPICE PORK TENDERLOIN

Makes 6 servings

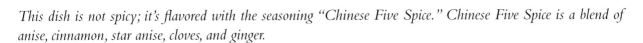

This dish is not spicy; it's flavored with the seasoning "Chinese Five Spice." Chinese Five Spice is a blend of anise, cinnamon, star anise, cloves, and ginger.

2½ lb. pork tenderloin (not center cut)
¼ cup soy sauce
3 Tbsp. honey
1 Tbsp. apple cider vinegar
3 Tbsp. water
1¼ tsp. Chinese Five Spice blend
2 garlic cloves, minced
2 tsp. cornstarch
Steamed rice for serving

Add the pork to a 5-quart or larger slow cooker.

In a small bowl whisk together soy sauce, honey, vinegar, water, Chinese Five Spice, garlic, and cornstarch; pour over the pork.

Cover and cook on LOW for 7–8 hours without opening the lid during cooking time.

Shred the meat with 2 forks. Serve over rice and top with sliced green onions.

DOUBLE PORK FRENCH DIPS

I know, I know, you're thinking: "Have some self-control, Sarah." But in all seriousness, these sandwiches are restaurant-level. The seasoned pork makes its own au jus for dipping, and the crunch from the bacon makes this the perfect sandwich.

1 tsp. salt
½ tsp. black pepper
1 tsp. onion powder
1 tsp. garlic powder
1 tsp. chili powder
⅛ tsp. cayenne pepper
3 lb. pork shoulder roast
2 Tbsp. canola or vegetable oil
2 (14.5-oz.) cans chicken broth
2 garlic cloves, minced

For Serving:
2 French bread baguettes, cut into six 5-inch servings
12 strips bacon, cooked
6 slices white cheddar cheese, cut in half diagonally

Mix the salt, pepper, onion powder, garlic powder, chili powder, and cayenne pepper in a small bowl. Rub this mixture all over the pork with clean hands. Put the cooking oil in large skillet set to medium–high heat; brown the meat on all sides. Place the browned roast into the slow cooker. Add one of the cans of chicken broth to the pan that the meat was browned in and scrape up the meaty bits and seasonings with a spatula. Pour this broth into the slow cooker, add the other can of broth, and place the chopped garlic on top of the roast.

Cover and cook on LOW for 8 hours without opening the lid during cooking time. Place the roast on a large sheet of foil and wrap up. Strain the au jus in the slow cooker by pouring it through a wire strainer into a large bowl, skim off fat of the au jus with a spoon, and then pour it back into the slow cooker.

Split the French bread rolls down the sides, open them up, pile up the meat, and top with cheese and bacon. Preheat the oven to broil at 500 degrees. Put the prepared sandwiches under the broiler in the oven for 3–7 minutes or until cheese is bubbly. Ladle the au jus into little bowls and serve.

ON-THE-GO PULLED PORK SANDWICHES

Makes 6 servings

On the nights our daughter has soccer lessons, we have about 30 minutes to get ready, eat dinner, and be out the door. These sandwiches are my go-to meal for these busy nights. Carrot sticks and grapes are an easy and healthy side for this sandwich.

4 lbs. pork shoulder roast
1 cup Sweet Baby Ray's barbecue Sauce
1 cup water
Buns and more barbecue sauce for serving

Place the roast in a 6-quart or larger slow cooker. Add the barbecue sauce on top of the roast, and add the water around the roast.

Cover and cook on LOW for 8–10 hours without opening lid during cooking time. Drain the fat and juices from the slow cooker.

Shred the meat with 2 forks, discarding any fatty pieces.

Toast the buns on the bagel setting of a toaster. Serve the shredded pork on the buns with barbecue sauce to taste.

BARBECUE PORK RIB TIPS

Makes 6 servings

Rib tips are a different cut of ribs; they have bone pieces instead of whole bones. They are a fun change from slab ribs, and they are less expensive too!

3 lbs. pork rib tips
2 Tbsp. brown sugar
½ tsp. black pepper
½ tsp. paprika
½ tsp. garlic powder
¼ tsp. onion powder
2 tsp. hickory liquid smoke
½ cup water
1 cup Sweet Baby Ray's barbecue sauce, divided

Combine the pepper, paprika, garlic powder, onion powder, and hickory liquid smoke in a small bowl and rub onto the ribs with clean hands. Place the ribs into a 6-quart slow cooker and brush with ½ cup of the barbecue sauce. Add the water around the ribs.

Cover and cook on LOW for 8–9 hours without opening the lid during the cooking time. Brush the remaining barbecue sauce on the ribs and serve. (Help little ones with these ribs, for the bone pieces could be choked on.)

Variation:

WHOLE RACK BABY BACK RIBS: On a large cutting board, remove the connective tissue that is on the back of the ribs by grabbing it on the top middle of the ribs and pulling; it should come off in one piece. Cut the ribs into four sections. Continue with the above recipe. (Makes 4 servings.)

PORK CHOPS, APPLES, AND CORNBREAD STUFFING

Makes 4 servings

I love a slow cooker dish that is almost a complete meal. Just add a salad or a steamed vegetable to this dish, and dinner is served.

1 (6-oz.) box Stove Top cornbread stuffing mix
1½ cups water
¼ cup butter, melted
1½ lbs. bone-in or thick-cut pork chops
1½ tsp. McCormick Montreal steak seasoning
2 Granny Smith apples, cored, peeled, and sliced
1 tsp. sugar
¼ tsp. cinnamon
4 strips bacon, cooked and crumbled

Spray a 6-quart oval slow cooker with nonstick cooking spray. Add the dry stuffing mix to the slow cooker. Drizzle the water and melted butter over the stuffing and stir. Sprinkle the pork chops on both sides with the steak seasoning and put on top of the stuffing.

In a small bowl, toss the apples with the sugar and cinnamon; place these and the bacon on top of the pork chops.

Cover and cook on LOW for 5 hours.

BLACK BEAN TOSTADAS

Makes 8 servings

You will not miss the meat with this meal! Creamy black beans on crunchy tostadas shells and served with your favorite toppings.

1 lb. dried black beans
5 cups water
¼ cup chopped cilantro
2 Tbsp. minced jalapeño
½ cup diced white onion
1 tsp. chili powder
⅛ tsp. pepper
1 tsp. salt (add to taste)
Tostada shells, lettuce, cheese, tomatoes, and avocados for serving

The night before, place the dried beans into a 6-quart slow cooker and cover with 4 inches of water. Let the beans soak overnight without turning the slow cooker on. Drain the beans in the morning. Add the 5 cups of fresh water, along with the rest of the ingredients except the salt and toppings.

Cover and cook on LOW for 10 hours. Remove half the beans and a few ladles of the bean liquid to a blender (secure the lid well and cover with towel to prevent possible burning); pulse until smooth. Add the puréed beans to the slow cooker with the remaining whole beans and stir. Add salt to taste.

Serve on warmed tostada shells topped with lettuce, cheese, tomatoes, and avocado.

NO-NOODLE ZUCCHINI LASAGNA

Makes 8 servings

Zucchini is cut lengthwise and acts as the noodles in this veggie lasagna. Still decadent and satisfying.

For the lasagna:
6 small zucchini
½ tsp. salt
2 cups shredded mozzarella
1 (24-oz.) jar marinara sauce (I use Newman's Own)

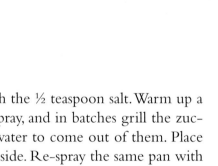

Ricotta mushroom filling:
2 cups diced mushrooms
1 (15-oz.) container part-skim ricotta
1 (5-oz.) container shredded parmesan
1 egg
½ tsp. salt
⅛ tsp. pepper

Slice the zucchini into ¼-inch slices lengthwise and sprinkle with the ½ teaspoon salt. Warm up a large nonstick skillet to medium-high heat, spray with nonstick spray, and in batches grill the zucchini for about 30 seconds on each side, just enough to get the water to come out of them. Place the zucchini on paper towels and blot the water out of them; set aside. Re-spray the same pan with nonstick spray and sauté the mushrooms until soft; drain and blot the mushrooms with a paper towel. Place the mushrooms into a large bowl and add the ricotta, Parmesan, egg, salt, and pepper; mix until combined.

Now, for the layering of the lasagna, add these layers in this order:

1. ⅓ jar of marinara

2. Layer of zucchini

3. ½ of the ricotta mushroom filling

4. ⅓ jar of marinara

5. Layer of zucchini

6. Other half of ricotta mushroom filling

7. Layer of zucchini

8. Last of marinara

9. Shredded mozzarella (all)

Cover and cook on HIGH for 2 hours. Open the lid and blot the water from top with a paper towel, cover, and continue cooking on HIGH for 30 more minutes.

Remove lid and let the lasagna rest for 30 minutes before serving.

VEGETARIAN PINTO BEANS OVER QUINOA

Makes 6 servings

My health-nut cousin made a version of this for a family get-together. I was pleasantly surprised how much I loved the quinoa and pinto bean combination. It is now a favorite meatless meal in our house.

For the beans:
1 lb. dried pinto beans
5 cups water
½ cup diced white onion
1 tsp. onion powder
1 tsp. oregano
1 tsp. chili powder
½–1 tsp. salt to taste

For the cilantro dressing:
¼ cup extra virgin olive oil
¼ cup freshly squeezed lime juice
¼ cup water
1 cup mayonnaise or plain Greek yogurt
2 cups cilantro leaves
¼ tsp. salt
⅛ tsp. pepper

Steamed quinoa, shredded red cabbage, and sliced cherry tomatoes for serving

Add the beans into a 6-quart slow cooker, add 4 inches of water above the beans, and soak overnight. Drain the beans in the morning and add the 5 cups of fresh water, onion, onion powder, oregano, and chili powder. Cover and cook on LOW for 10 hours. Add the cilantro lime dressing ingredients into a blender; pulse until smooth. Add the salt to taste to the beans and serve over quinoa with the cilantro dressing, shredded cabbage, and cherry tomatoes.

MARINARA PRIMAVERA

Makes 8 servings

I make this veggie sauce when my garden is going crazy, and it's such a great summer time meal. Light and fresh!

2 (28-oz.) cans crushed tomatoes
1 (6-oz.) can tomato paste
⅓ cup water
1 cup sliced carrots
½ cup diced white onion
1 garlic clove, minced
2 tsp. basil
2 tsp. oregano
½ tsp. salt
½ tsp. sugar
¼ tsp. crushed red pepper flakes
1 cup thinly sliced zucchini
1 cup thinly sliced yellow squash
1 cup halved cherry tomatoes
Cooked spiral-shaped noodles and Parmesan cheese for serving

Combine the crushed tomatoes, tomato paste, water, carrots, onion, garlic, and all the seasonings in a 6–quart slow cooker; stir.

Cover and cook on LOW for 8 hours without opening the lid during the cooking time.

Add zucchini and squash, cover and cook on HIGH for 1 hour more without opening the lid. Toss in cherry tomatoes and stir.

Serve over cooked noodles topped with freshly grated Parmesan.

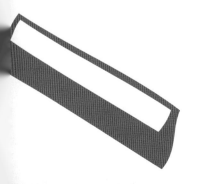

STUFFED POBLANO PEPPERS

Makes 4 servings

These stuffed poblano peppers are a complete Mexican meal; it tastes like chile rellenos with beans and rice. Some seriously good eats.

1 (16-oz.) jar salsa, divided
2 cups cooked and cooled rice
1 (15-oz.) can red beans, drained and rinsed
½ cup diced red onion
1 garlic clove, minced
½ tsp. salt
¼ tsp. pepper
⅛ tsp. cumin
4 poblano peppers
1 cup shredded cheddar cheese
Chopped cilantro for serving

Reserving ¼ cup salsa for the filling, add the rest of the jar to a 6-quart oval slow cooker. In a large bowl, combine the ¼ cup reserved salsa, rice, beans, garlic, salt, pepper, onion, and cumin.

Cut an oval shape from the top of the peppers and discard. Stuff the peppers with the filling. Place the stuffed peppers into the salsa in the slow cooker.

Cover cook on HIGH for 3 hours. Sprinkle the cheese onto the peppers and replace the lid until the cheese is melted.

Serve topped with chopped cilantro if desired.

DESSERTS

MACADAMIA NUT CLUSTERS

Makes 20 servings

These candies are fun to make for holiday cookie trays. You can make these while your oven is full of other goodies.

1 lb. macadamia nuts (I get these from the bulk section)
2 (12-oz.) pkgs. semisweet chocolate chips (I use Ghirardelli)
A pinch of salt

Add all ingredients to a 5-quart or larger slow cooker.

Cover and cook on LOW for 30–45 minutes, stirring every 10 minutes until the chocolate is melted.

Line a baking sheet with wax paper. Scoop the chocolate and nuts with a spoon or ice cream scoop that has a lever, about 2 tablespoons per cluster, onto the waxed cookie sheet.

Place in the refrigerator until set.

BLUEBERRY BUCKLE

Makes 6 servings

There is a blueberry farm just a half mile from our house. My daughter and I ride our bikes there every summer to pick berries and try our best not to spill them on our way home. This is our favorite recipe for those berries.

Layer 1:
1½ cups Bisquick baking mix
1 cup milk
¼ cup melted butter
2 Tbsp. sugar

Layer 2:
2 cups blueberries

Layer 3:
½ cup melted butter
½ cup brown sugar
3 Tbsp. flour

Vanilla ice cream for serving

In a small bowl, mix the "layer 1" ingredients until smooth. Spray a 6-quart oval slow cooker with nonstick spray. Smooth down this layer into the slow cooker, and then add the blueberries.

In another small bowl, combine the "layer 3" ingredients; crumble this mixture over the blueberries.

Cover and cook on HIGH for 2 hours.

Serve warm with vanilla ice cream.

CARAMEL APPLE CRISP

Makes 8 servings

I use a jarred caramel ice cream topping for the sauce: easy and delicious.

6 cups peeled and sliced Granny Smith apples
1 cup caramel sauce (jarred ice cream topping)
1½ cups standard oatmeal
½ cup flour
2 Tbsp. sugar
½ tsp. cinnamon
⅛ tsp. salt
½ cup melted salted butter
½ cup chopped walnuts
Ice cream for serving

Spray a 6-quart slow cooker with nonstick spray, add the sliced apples to the slow cooker in an even layer, and pour the caramel sauce over the apples.

In a small bowl, mix the oatmeal, flour, sugar, cinnamon, salt, and melted butter. Crumble this mixture over the apples and caramel, and then sprinkle the walnuts over the top.

Cover and cook on HIGH for 2½ hours.

Serve warm with vanilla ice cream.

CHEESECAKE

Makes 10 servings

Cheesecake in the slow cooker? Yes! It turns out creamy, and it doesn't crack on the top!

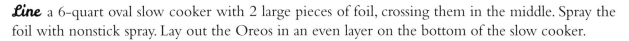

About 17 golden Oreos
3 (8-oz.) pkgs. cream cheese, room temperature
3 eggs
⅔ cup sugar
1 tsp. vanilla

Line a 6-quart oval slow cooker with 2 large pieces of foil, crossing them in the middle. Spray the foil with nonstick spray. Lay out the Oreos in an even layer on the bottom of the slow cooker.

In a large bowl, combine the cream cheese, eggs, sugar, and vanilla with an electric hand held mixer or a stand mixer fitted with the paddle attachment; blend the cream cheese mixture until smooth. Pour this over the Oreos in an even layer.

Cover and cook on HIGH for 1½ to 2 hours, until not jiggly in the center.

Turn off the slow cooker and let the cheesecake set up for 10 minutes. Carefully pull out the cheesecake by grabbing onto the foil and place on a cooling rack.

Place the cooling rack in the refrigerator and let the cheesecake chill for 2 hours before cutting.

STRAWBERRY RHUBARB CORNBREAD COBBLER

Makes 8 servings

This dessert is a favorite of mine. The cornbread topping complements the strawberries and rhubarb well.

2 (16-oz.) containers frozen sliced strawberries in sugar sauce, thawed
2 cups ½-inch slices of rhubarb
2 Tbsp. cornstarch
1 Jiffy corn muffin mix
1 egg
⅓ cup milk
1 Tbsp. sugar
¼ tsp. ground cinnamon
Vanilla ice cream for serving

Spray an oval 6-quart slow cooker with nonstick spray. Add the thawed strawberries, rhubarb, and cornstarch; stir until cornstarch is dissolved.

Mix the corn muffin mix, egg, and milk in a small bowl; pour and smooth this over the strawberry rhubarb mixture.

In a small bowl, combine the sugar and cinnamon; sprinkle on top of the cornbread mixture.

Cover and cook on HIGH for 2½ hours without opening the lid during the cooking time.

Serve warm with vanilla ice cream.

PUMPKIN CARAMEL FLAN

Makes 4 servings

These pumpkin flans are silky and luxurious, a wonderful dessert anytime of the year.

½ cup sweetened condensed milk
½ cup canned pumpkin purée
1 cup 2% milk
3 large eggs
½ tsp. pure vanilla extract
¼ tsp. ground cinnamon
A pinch of ground nutmeg
4 heaping Tbsp. caramel (jarred ice cream topping)
1 spray can whipped cream and nutmeg for serving

In a medium bowl, whisk together sweetened condensed milk, pumpkin, milk, eggs, vanilla, cinnamon, and nutmeg until smooth. Spread a heaping tablespoon of caramel syrup all over the inside of 4 (5-ounce) ramekins. Pour the flan mixture evenly into the caramel-coated ramekins. Add ½ inch of water to a 6-quart slow cooker and place the ramekins in the water.

Cover and cook on HIGH for 2–2½ hours without opening the lid during the cooking time. Peek at the flans through the lid; they are done when they have started to puff and are no longer jiggly in the center.

PEANUT BUTTER CHOCOLATE FONDUE

Makes 10 servings

Fondue is just plain exciting. I picked dipping items that can easily be dipped with hands, so you won't need skewers for this fondue.

For the Fondue:
1 (12-oz.) pkg. semi-sweet chocolate chips
1 cup creamy peanut butter

Dippers:
Large marshmallows
Nilla wafers
Strawberries
Sliced Granny Smith apples

Add the chocolate chips and peanut butter to a 2½-quart or larger slow cooker.

Cover cook on HIGH for 30–50 minutes, stirring every 10 minutes until smooth and melted.

Serve with dippers.

CHERRY CHIP JAR COOKIES

My mom would make cherry chip cake for every birthday for us four kids. The chopped cherries really liven up a boxed cake mix.

For the cakes:
1 cup white cake mix (from a 15.25-oz. boxed white cake mix)
⅓ cup water
2 Tbsp. canola or vegetable oil
1 egg
20 maraschino cherries

For the buttercream frosting:
½ cup salted butter (1 stick)
2 cups powdered sugar
½ tsp. pure vanilla extract
1 Tbsp. milk
A pinch of salt

In a medium-sized bowl, add the cake mix, water, oil, and egg; stir until combined. It's okay if some lumps are left. Put the maraschino cherries onto a cutting board and cut them into small pieces. Add to the cake batter and stir. Spray 8 (4-oz.) canning jars with nonstick spray and add the cake batter; there will be enough batter to fill the jars ⅓ full. Add the jars to a dry 6-quart slow cooker.

Cover and cook on HIGH for 2 hours without opening the lid during the cooking time.

Remove jars from the slow cooker with a potholder and place onto a cooling rack.

Add the butter, powdered sugar, and vanilla to a small bowl and beat together with a handheld mixer or a stand mixer fitted with the paddle attachment until blended. Add milk and continue mixing until smooth. Put the buttercream frosting into a piping bag (or a large Ziploc bag with the corner cut off) fitted with a 1M icing tip. When the cakes are completely cooled, pipe the frosting onto the cakes.

LIME BARS

Makes 10 servings

These bars are fun to make and pack a punch of lime flavor. I used pecan cookies for the crust. If you prefer, use another cookie such as golden Oreos.

About 13 pecan Sandies cookies
1 (14-oz.) can sweetened condensed milk
3 large eggs
1 Tbsp. lime zest
¼ cup lime juice
¼ tsp. pure vanilla extract
4 drops green food coloring (optional)
A pinch of salt

Line a 6-quart oval slow cooker with 2 long pieces of foil crossing each other; spray the insides of the foil with nonstick spray. Lay enough pecan cookies to cover the bottom of the slow cooker—some small spaces are okay.

Whisk together the rest of the ingredients in a medium bowl and place in the fridge for 20 minutes. Chilling this will thicken the filling enough so the cookies don't float when poured in. After the filling has chilled, pour the filling over the cookies.

Roll down the foil just enough to get the lid on. Cover and cook on HIGH for 1 hour and 45 minutes.

Remove the entire ceramic insert and place on a cooling rack for 20 minutes. Remove the lime bars by pulling on foil and place in the fridge on a cooling rack for at least 2 hours.

Cut into bars and serve.

PEACH COBBLER

Makes 8 servings

You can find Bisquick baking mix near the pancake mixes at the store. This mix makes a light and fluffy topping for the peaches.

For the filling:
2 (29-oz.) cans peaches in heavy syrup, 1 cup juices reserved
2 tsp. cornstarch
¼ tsp. ground cinnamon
2 tsp. sugar

For the Cobbler Topping:
1½ cups Bisquick baking mix
1 cup milk
¼ cup melted butter
1 Tbsp. sugar

For the topping:
1 Tbsp. sugar
¼ tsp. cinnamon

Add 1 cup peach juices from a can of the peaches into a medium-sized bowl, drain, and discard the rest of the juices. Add the cornstarch, ¼ teaspoon cinnamon, and 2 teaspoons sugar to the peach juices and whisk until smooth. Add in drained peaches and stir.

Spray a 6-quart slow cooker with nonstick spray and add peach mixture. In a small bowl, mix the cobbler topping ingredients until smooth and pour over peaches. Dust the top of the cobbler mixture with sugar and cinnamon.

Cover and cook on HIGH for 2½ hours without opening the lid during the cooking time.

CANDY BAR DIP

Makes 8 servings

This creamy caramel dip has pieces of Rolos and Heath bars stirred in. Fun for parties or gift-giving.

2 (14-oz.) cans sweetened condensed milk
2 (1.7-oz.) pkgs. Rolo candies, chopped
2 (1.4-oz.) pkgs. Heath chocolate toffee bars, chopped
Granny Smith apples for serving

Pour the sweetened condensed milk cans into a 3-quart or larger slow cooker.

Cover and cook on LOW for 45 minutes, occasionally stirring. Add the chopped candy bars into the warmed sweetened condensed milk and stir. Turn off slow cooker.

Serve promptly or ladle into 4-ounce jars for gift-giving.

LEMON SPOON CAKE

Lemon is my favorite dessert flavor. This cake is meant to be served warm with vanilla ice cream.

For the cake:
1 (15.25-oz.) box yellow cake mix
½ cup lemon juice
½ cup water
⅓ cup melted butter
3 eggs
1 Tbsp. lemon zest

For the glaze:
2 Tbsp. lemon juice
1 tsp. lemon zest
1 cup powdered sugar

For serving:
Vanilla ice cream

Spray a 6-quart slow cooker with nonstick cooking spray.

In a large bowl, combine the cake ingredients; mix until almost smooth; lumps are okay. Pour the batter into the slow cooker.

Cover and cook on HIGH for 2 hours. The cake is done when firm in the center.

Mix the glaze ingredients in a small bowl until smooth. Pour the glaze evenly over the cake and serve with vanilla ice cream.

COOKING MEASUREMENT EQUIVALENTS

Cups	Tablespoons	Fluid Ounces
⅛ cup	2 Tbsp.	1 fl. oz.
¼ cup	4 Tbsp.	2 fl. oz.
⅓ cup	5 Tbsp. + 1 tsp.	
½ cup	8 Tbsp.	4 fl. oz.
⅔ cup	10 Tbsp. + 2 tsp.	
¾ cup	12 Tbsp.	6 fl. oz.
1 cup	16 Tbsp.	8 fl. oz.

Cups	Fluid Ounces	Pints/Quarts/Gallons
1 cup	8 fl. oz.	½ pint
2 cups	16 fl. oz.	1 pint = ½ quart
3 cups	24 fl. oz.	1½ pints
4 cups	32 fl. oz.	2 pints = 1 quart
8 cups	64 fl. oz.	2 quarts = ½ gallon
16 cups	128 fl. oz.	4 quarts = 1 gallon

Other Helpful Equivalents

1 Tbsp.	3 tsp.
8 oz.	½ lb.
16 oz.	1 lb.

METRIC MEASUREMENT EQUIVALENTS

Approximate Weight Equivalents

Ounces	Pounds	Grams
4 oz.	¼ lb.	113 g
5 oz.		142 g
6 oz.		170 g
8 oz.	½ lb.	227 g
9 oz.		255 g
12 oz.	¾ lb.	340 g
16 oz.	1 lb.	454 g

Approximate Volume Equivalents

Cups	US Fluid Ounces	Milliliters
⅛ cup	1 fl. oz.	30 ml
¼ cup	2 fl. oz.	59 ml
½ cup	4 fl. oz.	118 ml
¾ cup	6 fl. oz.	177 ml
1 cup	8 fl. oz.	237 ml

Other Helpful Equivalents

½ tsp.	2½ ml
1 tsp.	5 ml
1 Tbsp.	15 ml

INDEX

ABOUT THE AUTHOR

SARAH OLSON is the creator of the blog *The Magical Slow Cooker*. She loves that a few simple ingredients can turn into magic while slow cooking. Sarah also works full-time as a mail carrier and resides in Springfield, Oregon, with her husband and young daughter. You can learn more about Sarah at www.themagicalslowcooker.com.